praise for Darren C. Demaree

"Darren C. Demaree's collection is a blanketed conversation with a dear friend. *in defense of the goat that continues to wander towards the certain doom of the cliff* meanders and weaves—Demaree is a philosopher who confronts our 'imperiled belief / that knowledge grazes this world / without falling off this world.' In this novel in verse, each poem searches for meaning, each poem is a universe that demands we 'view the world view the word view the world.' This is a collection of the imagination, a collection that insists 'we can belong in this world' and there is a 'joy that comes with flapping one's arms.'"
– Allison Blevins, author of *Cataloguing Pain*

"*in defense of the goat that continues to wander towards the certain doom of the cliff* is a radical, brilliant masterclass in metaphor, a collection of poems that engages deeply with the 'vital kinship of the invisible empire.' Every poem here begins and ends where 'two-thirds of the landscape / has been ruined and two-thirds / of the animals are unknown.' These poems are brief, mighty and bold; they ground us while insisting that our imaginations must not be forsaken and that we must not be at odds with the world around us. Darren C. Demaree invites readers into 'the remaining wilderness' which is being 'asked / to grow a fungus that can save us.' When we find 'too much god in the honey,' how can we remain rooted? If 'life is a miracle that can't / fly,' *in defense of the goat that continues to wander towards the certain doom of the cliff* shows us how to go as far as we can on foot."
– Joan Kwon Glass, author of *Night Swim*

"Demaree's collection reads like an extended surrealist aphorism—one that thickly describes 'this place we have all seen,' a precarious world that increasingly reveals itself to be 'adaptative as in refusing / to be the end even if it is / the end of our understanding.' Demaree articulates across this book as much a poetics as an ethics of creation, of 'obligation' to nature that is itself poetry constantly unfolding as much as the rational and the empirical might want to disavow. 'i'm telling you the science / needs the poetry as much as we need the science,' Demaree's speaker urgently proclaims. We ought to heed this, now more than ever in our troubled present."
– Travis Chi Wing Lau, author of *Paring* and *Vagaries*

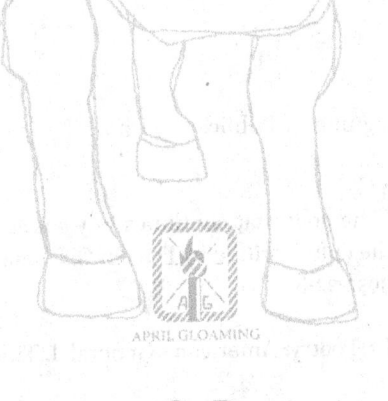

in defense of the goat that continues to wander towards the certain doom of the cliff

Darren C. Demaree

Publisher's Cataloguing-in-Publication Data

Demaree, Darren C.
    In defense of the goat that continues to wander towards the certain doom of the cliff / written by Darren C. Demaree
    ISBN: 978-1-953932-22-8

1. Poetry: General 2. Poetry: American - General I. Title
II. Author

Library of Congress Control Number: 2023950652

*This book is dedicated to public library workers everywhere,
but especially to the many splendid folks
at the Columbus Metropolitan Library system.*

invested in the principal
that grass allowed to grow
will eventually melt
in a mouth of free teeth
is the only real intimacy
the moment the animal
decides to consume
the landscape cannot be
reduced to a checklist
cannot hold steady
for the gaze of humanity
which only sees the tail move

**in defense of the goat that continues to wander
towards the certain doom of the cliff**

it's not all a multilevel selection
the forever conflict the queen
of the moment the dirt as
an operating table of the scene
where the highly-readable destiny
is read out loud is a momentum
thud a revolt against the happening
which will always happen
the tide is never not the tide
even if the moon crashed into
the cliff the salt would find the goat
with great eloquence it would care

this place we have all seen
adaptative as in refusing
to be the end even if it is
the end of our understanding
the northern reaches
of our imperiled belief
that knowledge grazes this world
without falling off this world
& then again the immensity
of us imagining a fall
that can never end a spirit
as light as an invention

**in defense of the goat that continues to wander
towards the certain doom of the cliff**

there's a tick an american history
that will tell you there are fifty
bodies without faces at the bottom
of the cliff in the rocks they are
the rocks they will tell you the salt
keeps them to trample them
as is the way in every nation state
in earlier times now now in future times
the goat full-mouthed or empty will
look down at the human wreckage modern
as urgency to make it to the edge
of humanity to watch another decision

the light is unconscious noticed
away from the cutting edges
of the chemical alarms lemony
in the filter narrow in the worst wild
what flying makes gravity worth
the countlessly various deaths
of simple creatures of prophetic
humans that can only predict death
show me an endgame that is
a beginning show me a brave
expression a program dispersed
a lack of conquest a life on this earth

in defense of the goat that continues to wander towards the certain doom of the cliff

this is ohio let's say it was a rhino
that escaped from one of our plights
a zoo that is both gun and germ
& iron ticket-booth but now a rhino
has made it to the water's edge has charged
past the grass past the witnesses
to prove that life is a miracle that can't
fly that can't believe into flight a half-
despair half-vision an achievable plan
if the plan is to watch a rhino refuse
to pause at the presence of the ocean
because we told it we were the ocean

the protein is a limit the oxygen isn't
the future is only alertness unwrapped
while we box up obfuscation again
& good lord tell me once more why
the remaining wilderness is being asked
to grow a fungus that can save us
that can mean human existence can be
carried beneath a tree while we harvest
all the trees i am as knowledgeable
as a common man that believes in science
i can't tell you why we placed the hook
inside our mouths called ourselves planners

in defense of the goat that continues to wander
towards the certain doom of the cliff

there is no new goat each transition
is a gravel pit each blade of grass
tucked away for the future life
of the same animal the agitated mercy
the ten stars of our hope shining without
a culture of survival they die they die
slow enough for their light to find us
amidst the belief of the belief those many
names for our surface tension the laws
that keep us on the surface of the planet
& own us the same way every law owns
ask the field how much it cares ask

all mobilization is spiritual the peach cannot
roll into the conquest of the mouth it wants to
life is a miracle that way we learn the surface
of the selection when we are selected the creativity
the sun is in the moon how daring of a theory
that there is evidence of creation still amidst
the final stages of sanity the saving people still
talk about the eloquence is gone thank the bloom
the eloquence is gone the impulse to protect
the vital kinship of the invisible empire the invisible
artist the invisible rhythm all layers themselves
each a better way when smashed against it all

**in defense of the goat that continues to wander
towards the certain doom of the cliff**

a fable a folly a fable a folly
the inexpressible feeling
of an experience with salt
instruments with accumulation
the future it cannot be
a bottle we hold life isn't
a bottle we hold life isn't
the future it cannot be
instruments with accumulation
of an experience with salt
the inexpressible feeling
a fable a folly a fable a folly

there is a narrow understanding of the rest
of the nothing it could even be everything
the truth is nonetheless dammit that is so
science is a miracle dammit we developed
a world after we were given a world the two
cultures of falling and falling again all rest
to ride on the consequence of before us they ran
into the sea with many names on their tongue
with one name on their tongue with calamity
filling their lungs the dead shared too much
death with us the discovery that we loved
the dead anyway kept us from hating the tide

**in defense of the goat that continues to wander
towards the certain doom of the cliff**

the artist is multiple images multiple wants
a laboratory studies promise laid bare
on a bloom that might never find the color
to combat the wind let's say knowledge is life
& the desire to consume life is the origin
which god wants to tuck us into their cheek
the goat is coming with us which god wants
more than we do we stand up we leap
we use profanity all the fucking time which
condition of our origin will vacate the ultrafine
sheen we leave against the teeth of this world
the masterwork is that we believe in time at all

the ocean is vulgar only because we open
our mouths for salt whenever we get
a chance to drown in the taste of loyal
tears those clingers to the sad question
brilliant as it is does drowning feel worse
if the meaning of human existence is not
to fight for more meaning than existence
there is the releaser the gigantic nod
to odor i have watched everything degrade
so what we stink the ocean can do what
to our skin other than keep it that promise
is similar to flight is better than religion

in defense of the goat that continues to wander towards the certain doom of the cliff

time & after time the destruction of integrity
applies mostly to solid matter though sub-length
half-earth non-fighting humans become cavity
become sink-holes for the rest of the legged
powers they subtract trust that the water will
catch us if we leap that our burials matter
regardless of their physical state that is all to say
there are too many people leaving raspberries
on the skin of a prophet's arm to build much here
no matter no matter no matter the truth is told
in the tradition of surviving up until the cliff
& the joy that comes with flapping one's arms

in a time of need the goat enables us
an independent reality a promise
to be tightly packed grains a stalk
of the half-bloom an increasingly clear
& blank future blank in meaning as now
is blank in meaning though four legs
milling about the danger of our fractions
our factions our land that gives in to sea
our air which lords over us to burn in
our attention those four legs are key
the grass is treasure even the shit in
the grass is a biological promise it is

in defense of the goat that continues to wander towards the certain doom of the cliff

over an extended grind the bottle's neck
always shatters the superorganism wilts
at the glimpse of the new origin be be be
creative with it the animal loss includes us
that does not mean we should encourage
the dark wavelength the cliff calls it only
becomes more cliff that does not mean
we must wager on wings the tradition is
that we look for prophets that never works
besides we know the future we must change
the future speak it calmly the solution
is wholly unthought now this is wilderness

the order is insect arachnid ant bee wasp spider
the order is a mafia let them do what they want
with the fish with the horse's head with us
our open mouths our red squares that always
threaten evolution that never evolve that mutate
inversely searching the back of the throat for reasons
there is a tongue wagging in the monochromatic
light of human tissue cast back & forth like a flag
for a nation of neverwells let all that buzzing make
a home in us at the cellular level the advance away
from abstract thought might ruin the arts for a bit
but really that tenderness is so damn scattershot

in defense of the goat that continues to wander towards the certain doom of the cliff

sure reductionism is a threat to the last
half-century the discoverer of less would
stand in defiance of the good lord give me
the wealth-drowning i prefer there is a need
to count everything so that we ourselves might
be counted our survival broadened
into meaning the conservation efforts
focus on conserving humanity i tell you
it will be a different kind of okay if we don't
survive but it will be okay think of the gods
without our idea of the gods making life
a half-prison what limits what limits what

there is no reason to assume the languages
will fail us look into the eyes of the living
it's discovery every time that won't dampen
or disqualify the explicitly of this world
the only part of this that has no meaning
is the business part of this if we must be used
let us be used by something with eyes
a breathing focus the reclamation of the shore
the profanity of joy the everything for nothing
hold the motion of this world in your cheek
try not to weep every father is blind move
away it's necessary to leave death as a man

**in defense of the goat that continues to wander
towards the certain doom of the cliff**

overgrown those who have learned to absorb
the rendering of a philosophy based on reality
being the underlining punch of true wonder
will always remain overconfident that their body
matters that their body in the apprehension
of beauty it's organic to feel your cells dying
& paint over that idea to make art of the idea
& forge ahead to death's confrontation remove
that idea the grand result of our discipline is that
there is only the goat standing in the wind while
the plastic chokes off the sea true beauty is when
the problems demand an answer we answer

the neglect is all cavalry the horse
that loses the rider doesn't attempt
to fly over the ocean the horse with
the weight of our intentions never
eats freely again becomes more
metaphor than horse this is the part
where the only clear idea to consider
is that freeing all of the horses might
redeem humanity but really it would
only lead to fewer horse's carcasses
being filled by crabs if this finds you
mid-air on a horse dammit turn around

in defense of the goat that continues to wander
towards the certain doom of the cliff

the following way augments the spirit
makes numbers out of all of us heavens
the context right off of this world kills
the pattern of charges makes us less
responsible for the existence that stems
to bloom all around us there are larger moons
than ours languages in the better picture
of the universe that we don't yet speak
& yet we imagine paradise in human ways
hundreds of millions of years have led
to no new elements only our refusal to hold
an honest effort the while oxygen kisses us

the present claims everything
& without a eusociality
for our souls we are left
to watch for a second phenomenon
as if there is more religion
than the goat the cliff the sea
& the slight air that separates
them so lovingly that death
as all death will simply be
the return of the return
of the return we are witnesses
as in we are seldom noticed

in defense of the goat that continues to wander
towards the certain doom of the cliff

the red zone the clear cut the clearing
water beneath the dry scene a landscape
willing to fold into itself like a promise
& a theory colliding into the horizon
of course there is a reason to work human
thighs up a dramatic cliffside for no reason
other than to feature our legs in the wind
where there is only what can be picked up
& carried never filtered a charismatic
meeting we call the future includes us only
when we work to join it it's usually rare
we can belong in this world we almost do

our impairment our separation the drifting
to drift away it all ends without a meaning
the north water never stays the north water
but that is not the point reality is simpler
if you ignore the cult-leaders look up look
sideways face flush to the green provocation
the creativity that comes that we plant upon
the plants is why we have a relation to this world
we can all imagine the bloom without seeing
the health of the roots sure look to the moon
if you're sleeping on the hill look to the horizon
if you wake up look for the river if you dream

in defense of the goat that continues to wander
towards the certain doom of the cliff

i find nothing wrong with the grass
i find nothing wrong with the goat
i find nothing wrong with the cliff

i find nothing wrong with gravity
i find nothing wrong with the rocks
i find nothing wrong with the seafoam

i find nothing wrong with the tide
i find nothing wrong the taking
i find nothing wrong with the moon

i wish there were a better metaphor
& i wish the goat knew really knew
how much i absolutely adore its bell

none of the insects look over the cliff
& go over the cliff it takes real art to eat
into gravity to be lost in gravity death
is not art though ruin is not art unless
you're ruining the meal of the watchers
i want the cliff so i can look over the cliff
so i can follow the goat with my eyes
& my wishes my natural fires my desire
to find a world beyond belief so save this
world that cannot exceed belief please
be a butterfly if you can take the edge
as the edge if you can't stop pushing stop

**in defense of the goat that continues to wander
towards the certain doom of the cliff**

the skin of the water doesn't reach
only splashes the skin of the goat
does nothing but hold onto the goat
our skin is shed like a snake's when
the rose bush promises us tenderness
the jaws of the world all of the jaws
of the world open to never close again
the snow cannot hold on the expression
of the snow can only be loss the cold
is pure the heat muddled the living
consider it a career the best students
are the roots destroying us to live on

toe hair nipple canopy the crows
the population of any moment
grows with our understanding
of that moment the future is not
always the future if we're talking
about the meaning of the future
each small pocket each tiny heart
of the semiwild are myth-worthy
& then in the telling they are myth
that is how reality becomes big
enough for a response to the heat
of this world it's the expression

in defense of the goat that continues to wander
towards the certain doom of the cliff

hours the ambush the bacteria
& the blood rest on the enchantment
of everything on this planet spreads
the goat drags everything with it
the color is a root structure blooming
into certainty what unique what unique
evolution only the small hooves refusing
to rest in the puddle gives us hope
only the celebration that conservation
& conservatism are highly readable
& only one of them is dead destiny how
unlimited an animal without bullets is

a body a reservoir a movement
a tendency to modify the perfection
of then of now of when will we
take a whole hour to describe
the small group of us that watch
the goat without ever touching
the goat as if allowing that skin
to fail to kite in the moon-context
will save us from our own sacrifices
let us be saved by understanding
that creation can be a better story
if it doesn't end where the grass ends

in defense of the goat that continues to wander
towards the certain doom of the cliff

from the town to the edge of the town
to where the land ends back to the town
& such imitation is pleasant enough
we carry too rarely from we carry we carry
when our hands are free we find ways
to love even a pencil in the hand can
take a half-dozen living things as distraction
let's say we want to be heard but all we do
is carry let's say the screaming on the beach
is the other way the screaming in the town
is the other way do not be afraid of it all
be loud be free be love that is never routine

two-thirds of the landscape
has been ruined two-thirds
of the animals are unknown
i don't think we should know
everything i don't think we
should be everywhere be
daring quiet lost lost lost okay
in the lack of hallmark daring
in this will never be remembered
there is a philosophy in stillness
the water cannot be diverted
forever this is a wonderful place

**in defense of the goat that continues to wander
towards the certain doom of the cliff**

four birds a prediction an expectation
there are no berries this close to the sea
aren't there berries this close to the sea
an attempt an invitation the refusal
of the tree to have a family of roots
& give nothing there must be berries
this close to the sea those birds look
like migrating birds they are here in
the chill all four of them with different
colors all red with anticipation us our hands
run against the framework asking if we
ever know truly about what makes a berry

come contemplation this spectacular
education is desperate enough to make
us measure the land the water the air
a second time it's true so very true
a full burial of truth the cup of leaves
spread over our studies thinly the cup
of salt the origin of all this meaning
spread into the post-history where we
will exist only in molecular beauty
a scar on the remaining depth
of the sequence all the falling will
stop until there can be a new falling

in defense of the goat that continues to wander towards the certain doom of the cliff

we have an obligation
to the springtails the grass
the red-knobbed beaks
the indecipherable force
that traces this day into
the next the previously gone
& the view that we were
never really here anyway
i'm telling you the science
needs the poetry as much
as we need the science the cliff
is a goddamn villanelle

view the world view the world view the world
a worldview is a half-earth compared to keeping
your eyes open such an idea is nineteenth century
alas your conquest is worthless if you're conquered
by the notes of the hopeless the tenor of hatred
the slaughtering of the goat before the goat can
splash mangled social absolutely inimitable you
founders that only find the path you're on what joy
what joy the truth is almost always elsewhere
a new truth is always elsewhere if you can avoid
the colonial then you can hold the berries eat only
what you need juice nothing all that wasted skin

in defense of the goat that continues to wander
towards the certain doom of the cliff

the old anxiousness that god was
going to move our planet from one
ear to another ear has been replaced
by the anxiousness that the god
we imagined only ever consumed
& shat because we as human beings
rarely do more than consume
& shit so what miracle is this life
now now now the fear that even fear
is wholly imagined that energy jumps
the channel to run through unachievable
plans is conviction is our jeremiad

traced further & further back the pain
variety sunlight-driven the origin of forcing
the confines of this world the poverty
of being given everything told by bodies
that we're given just enough neurons
& pain receptors to feel the dying soon
as we're born we were born as a future
& we became watchers of the future teeth
that gnashed regardless of the full plate
our species oversimplified by desires when
asking questions is our greatest gift ask
the wind anything you will get an answer

in defense of the goat that continues to wander
towards the certain doom of the cliff

please think again the obliteration
of human eloquence is not an actual
loss a single grunt can be a song
if someone else hears it the massive
damage we've done here cannot be
fixed by a lyric listen to the millions
of bird as they fly away from our tide
be the brave expression of we can only
think to breathe clearly again without
the threat of the central question imploding
in our chests lower yourself think survival
first please please please think again

the arts have been divided
between those that know
the goat is meant to be
beautiful meant to be brave
meant to die with saltwater
filling each spectacular wound
& those that believe it will fly
if we describe the landscape
in a way that explodes
the frame that makes note
of death but never gives in
that edge is real what else

in defense of the goat that continues to wander
towards the certain doom of the cliff

the cliff isn't proportional to the drama
of the imagination it takes to give simplicity
to the cliff animal to animal to animal
we want powerful explanations we want
flesh to be more than flesh we want flight
to be unresolved unresolvable a tension
the selfishness can level all knowledge
the philosophers give us nothing
they don't want back the paintings all hide
too much from the children the nests
are the hallmark of curiosity that tree
each trunk is enough culture for the year

above the ocean in the ocean
on the way to meeting the ocean
we spend too much time considering
the rocks as our future of life
consequently we spend hamstrings
slowly we flex to fly almost never
& i know there is already mythology
fighting against creativity why why
believe in the group-level selection
when the origin considered nothing
but the singular existence no no
when we breathe in we breathe it all

**in defense of the goat that continues to wander
towards the certain doom of the cliff**

not for a specific life or conquest
of miracle but for the assemblage
the village the city that spills onto
the coast the revolutionary walking
the other way creatures that fly
over machines through machines
dying in machines us their masters
inept in their world i want one
moment of limitless nature i know i don't
belong in most of the times i imagine
such greenery i don't picture myself
i know better i want to know better

the rule follows the fear the fear
follows the misinterpretation
the misinterpretation follows
the meaning of human existence
the meaning of human existence
is a false flag operation be with
the deer be with the ten thousand
birds native to the cliff encourage
the goat encourage life to run
rampant the results of each mistake
made when you are with deer
with birds the goat are the wind

**in defense of the goat that continues to wander
towards the certain doom of the cliff**

the sound has a meaning why
granted the pond holds many
stones many rings a lot of shit
that holds a degree of kinship
with humanity no sounds come
from the bottom of the pond
though so does the tree listen
after the splash does the fox
allow both eyes to waver from
the hindlegs of the goat which
splash will mean the absolute
end give attention give more

i know which is to say i have failed
on many mornings when i chose
to force an understanding of the mystery
i could create that i could make larger
than myself forced myself to tell everyone
else what it is i had figured out which
was no miracle other than a tuesday
which is the least like any real miracle
that can be found i spoke loudly
when i didn't need to speak at all
i could not help myself it felt like it was
my time to cloud the thickening horizon

**in defense of the goat that continues to wander
towards the certain doom of the cliff**

semiwild the spikes of the open
sea are never experimental
watch the bowing drag us back
to the old conquests of this world
over the new world over bodies
strewn strolling into death
without imagining the formation
we could fix if we all fell off
the cliff if we followed away
from the furrow if we gave the goat
more than our imagination culture
bends with the light every time

the interaction with the goat
will not stall the goat will not
create new life for the goat will
not synthesize a more meaningful
death for the goat speak freely
at all times the end is the end
we should have never treated
this landscape like it could
never be the end we kept shoving
frames against the frailty called
it beauty every time spoke
longingly about restraint damn

**in defense of the goat that continues to wander
towards the certain doom of the cliff**

what of the wolves the wolves
exclaim loudly in a story about
the origin of the wolves the end
of the wolves where they are
never defeated where they eat
themselves to death all of them
men consuming as conquest
servants of this terrible conquest
here is the key to humanity
the wolves never leap off the cliff
they'd rather play in shit if
the shit reminds them of a meal

this setting commands the soul
of a biologist to work past understanding
& the soul of a poet to remove
the idea that poets have souls
that souls unlike poetry are not
the best of ideas that they give cover
to the immediate destruction
of the whole spiderweb of existence
we don't project off planet or plane
we don't move beyond the numbers
or the genetic coding it ends that is
beautiful it's ending that is terrible

**in defense of the goat that continues to wander
towards the certain doom of the cliff**

the village can no longer scatter
we are up against the field party
that leads to snack grass the goat
that exists because we dared
to believe we might want to create
a super-world that couldn't be eaten
with it all teethed couldn't be eaten
with good evil lost all sporting
teeth couldn't be eaten what future
involves absentia what future
will involve our will our will is done
& i so badly want to want nothing

let all the explanations be joined
so they can leap off the cliff together
are we saving ourselves or are we
waiting to be buried where we fall
feel no hesitation feel no fear feel
feel feel the wind is rushing the sun
has broken through the temperature
is too warm too cold too too too
& we understand only the errors
of the past make it the whole modern
economy saving listening an empathy
for the future the full field of hope

in defense of the goat that continues to wander
towards the certain doom of the cliff

chestnuts white fur all that death tastes
the consilience of the living and the story
of the living atoms morphing posing
for each other surviving a new synthesis
losing oxygen in drips the heat the heat
every heartfelt plea by the countless shapes
around our campsite knee problems
cracked teeth wolf wounds valleys of dark
earth waiting for the abundance
the patience that comes with a future
the shortfall the shortfall let me tell you
a story about when we got real creative

i have watched the path of the ants
entirely distinguish themselves by leaving
the city building during the field party
approaching the cliff without fear walking
down the side climbing the rocks at the entrance
of the sea provide the expression of all time
to the coming tide eloquent
& important in their deaths their living
so dynamic that i for the first time
felt i would like to be buried in a hole
without a casket i want the ants to carry me
to the sand in pieces let that be my enchantment

in defense of the goat that continues to wander
towards the certain doom of the cliff

the message is rarely timely the animals
don't raise their heads for a message
the whole roster of creatures is thinking of eating
now now now the snowflakes arrive to melt
the education begins in the belly
don't let that lower you your esteem
for the whole ecosystem we all must eat we
all must be ready not to eat individually
our saving will be to learn the value of hunger
collectively we must learn to leave the honey
where it is there is too much god in the honey
in the making of the honey the perfect drip of it

leave food for the thin birds
make it hard to imagine the song
fading let the truth deal with
the truth it could be a millennia
without us we could return maybe
as a new species there is no heaven
in that blink but do we care
about a heaven without thin birds
we cannot forge ahead anyway we
can only learn to sing old songs
& make out a little bit with biology
& the gift of matter mattering

**in defense of the goat that continues to wander
towards the certain doom of the cliff**

the logic is clear our position relies
too much on the existence of angels
& less on the belief that the goat's time
has always been of use the goat wanders
as we fear we fear we fear we isolate
during the stroll to the burning of our time
& we fear we fear we fear that this
is metaphor allusion illusion computer
antics god antics a universe's rage
a long tradition of losing control
chaos of an untender nature strange
support for our demise our anomaly

told here low to the ground the chewing
of the grass is a small cost for imagination
a personal cost for the continued imagination
we get surprised all the time by the leaps
we take the originality of our defense of love
or permanent death the bees that sting us
& die to give us real guilt the world that crumbles
into cliffsides too often flight that fails
when we need it to fail skeletons skeletons
the ransacking is almost done what can we pile
what can we lose which stories can we carry
& fear learn from embrace wait with until until

acknowledgments

Some of the individual poems in this book have appeared in *Coffin Bell, Descant, Digging Through the Fat, the Dillydoun Review, Doubly Mad, Eclectica, The Laurel Review,* and *Lost Pilots.*

author bio

Darren C. Demaree grew up in Mount Vernon, Ohio. He is a graduate of the College of Wooster, Miami University, and Kent State University. He is the recipient of a Greater Columbus Arts Council Grant, an Ohio Arts Council Individual Excellence Award, the Louise Bogan Award from Trio House Press, and the Nancy Dew Taylor Award from *Emrys Journal*. He is the Editor-in-Chief of the Best of the Net Anthology and Managing Editor of Ovenbird Poetry. He is currently working in the Columbus Metropolitan Library system, and living in Columbus, Ohio with his wife and children. *in defense of the goat as it continues to wander towards the certain doom of the cliff* is his twenty-first full-length collection of poetry.